WORSHIP
Keys

for Worthful Living

Andrew Allans Mutambo

WORSHIP KEYS

For Worthful Living
Copyright © Andrew Allans Mutambo,
All rights reserved,
Printed in the United States

Rivendell Publishing

www.rivendellpublishing.com

ORGINAL LAYOUT DESIGN & PRINT:
Anthony Saint
for Illustria
Nairobi, Kenya
+254 722 102232/ +256 779 982377
tony.saint30@gmail.com

To order copies online visit:
www.andrewmutambo.com

To schedule a speaking engagement or for
more information contact:

Andrew Mutambo

P.O BOX 22292

KAMPALA, UGANDA.
U.S. Line: 1-804-601-0394

Ugandan Line: (256)-772-404389

Email: andymutts@gmail.com

Dedication

To all whose hearts and lips are never somber to the sound of worship. Who find it hard to keep silent on the sidewalks, in their living rooms and washrooms. Who are found singing to themselves and by themselves in their kitchens, offices and business premises; making melody to their King in season and out. Whose voices affix value to the bumpy surroundings of life; passionate about seeing the fallen tabernacle of David reinstated within them and in every other soul. To all subscribing to this call, welcome to the world of worship!

Introduction

The inspiration to pen down this manuscript comes from a season of worship thoughts that have through the years been pouring into my heart. These ideas I consider so rich and profound have propelled me to unselfishly express myself in a manner that will uplift and enlighten my readers about the beauty, benefits and bountifulness of worship. Take time in your bed over a cup of coffee or on your couch with a friend and meditatively soak in these concepts. They will inspire and revitalize your life. Never forget it's an honor to worship God.

Revelations 1:10-18

I was in the Spirit on the Lord's day, and heard behind me a great voice, as of a trumpet,

Saying, I am Alpha and Omega, the first and the last: and, What thou seest, write in a book, and send it unto the seven churches which are in Asia; unto Ephesus, and unto Smyrna, and unto Pergamos, and unto Thyatira, and unto Sardis, and unto Philadelphia, and unto Laodicea.

And I turned to see the voice that spake with me. And being turned, I saw seven golden candlesticks;

And in the midst of the seven candlesticks one like unto the Son of man, clothed with a garment down to the foot, and girt about the paps with a golden girdle.

His head and his hairs were white like wool, as white as snow; and his eyes were as a flame of fire;

And his feet like unto fine brass, as if they burned in a furnace; and his voice as the sound of many waters.

And he had in his right hand seven stars: and out of his mouth went a sharp twoedged sword: and his countenance was as the sun shineth in his strength.

And when I saw him, I fell at his feet as dead. And he laid his right hand upon me, saying unto me, Fear not; I am the first and the last:

I am he that liveth, and was dead; and, behold, I am alive for evermore, Amen; and have the keys of hell and of death.

WORSHIP KEY # 1

Worship reveals the deepest form of our love!

Love is a seed having its origin in God. Man by nature is selfish and greedy. As we genuinely begin to worship God, we tap into the hesed/agape love embedded in us; enabling us express authentic, honest and sacrificial affection for God.

WORSHIP KEY # 2

Worship is a faith booster; it discovers faith and decimates fear!

Faith is foundational in our Christian livelihood. This faith however wanes. Worship creates the atmosphere in which our faith is revamped and resuscitated enabling us to bounce back, ready for another victorious day.

WORSHIP KEY # 3

Worship is God's love revealed and released back to HIM.

The only way you and I can render due homage to God for his eternal love is in our worship. It's here that we learn to give back to God for all, through all and in all that he is, has been and will do in our lives.

WORSHIP KEY # 4

Worship is the highest form of spiritual intercourse; cultivated in 'high-places'.

There is no greater form of interaction one can have with God save through worship; because there-in a cavernous and complex bond of intimacy is woven and fused between bride and groom.

WORSHIP KEY # 5

Worship is the antidote for doubt and unbelief.

Pressures of life are a consistent and unavoidable element of nature. A life of worship will always be a vanguard against the marauding spirits that are out to deflate your promised joy and happiness in God.

WORSHIP KEY # 6

Worship gives you private audience with the king.

Nothing wins the heart of a king like eulogy and gratitude. God's heart is eternally hard-wired to spontaneously tune into a heart of worship; warranting it special status before his throne.

WORSHIP KEY # 7

Worship is our heart's love letter whose vernacular and vocabulary only God understands!

In moments of our deepest weakness, utter perplexity or overwhelming happiness, the vocalization and expressions of our worship are a modulation only God can pick and make out.

WORSHIP KEY # 8

Worship isn't for our enjoyment but Enactment.

Many would confuse our form with our function. In worship God is the recipient and we the donors. We don't enjoy a worship service; inversely God does. Instead we are blessed to be of service to HIM in those moments.

WORSHIP KEY # 9

Worship is a public declaration of a private discovery and discourse.

Anything one dearly loves, they are compelled to chatter about. An encounter with God in worship creates an insatiable longing to be with and afterwards make him a topical issue to others.

WORSHIP KEY # 10

Worship is an expression of a selfless heart, demonstrated through our spirit and soul faculties; evidenced by our body language.

Every part of our lives was created to serve God. Learning to harmonize all our members in worship, begets an awareness of the splendor of the manufacturer and the beauty of his model.

WORSHIP KEY # 11

Prayer moves the hand of God; Worship moves his heart!

God has bound himself to listen and act on our prayer. On the other hand, in worship, his heart reaches out beyond our deepest imagination and desires fulfilling his intended purpose for us.

WORSHIP KEY # 12

Worship is about
thanks-living and thanks-
giving; an embodiment
of singing, shouting,
clapping, jumping,
dancing, recitation,
laughing, loving and
giving. All this done with a
spiritual vibe.

WORSHIP KEY # 13

Worship is the currency for God`s presence; through it we exchange our gloom for his glory.

Underscoring the power of worship will leap frog you from your pit to your pinnacle. Ideally you can't help but leave your baggage at his feet and embrace your blessing on the way out.

When your worship increases in stature, your status changes.

The attitude of worship is a spring board to a new altitude. A resolute and relentless engagement therein magnifies your creator to a point where your cremator is totally diminished.

WORSHIP KEY # 15

A worshipper learns to retrace their footsteps to the place of their first love.

Every cascade of our worship is meant to reveal his mercy and grace. Mercy is a pointer to a sinner saved by grace; Grace is a cursor to a saint washed by his blood.

The mark of a worshipper is his response during life's hardest storms.

Whining and whimpering is not the lingua franca of a worshipper. His stress code in dire circumstances is, "I will bless the Lord at all times, his praise shall continuously be on my lips."

WORSHIP KEY # 17

Worship begets the wisdom to respond in peculiar moments.

During seasons of worship, streams of divine wisdom surge from the throne room coming as keys to decipher the complex situations we face and provide us a way of escape.

WORSHIP KEY # 18

Worship is therapeutic to our lives massaging our mental and spiritual faculties!

Worship triggers all our faculties into play. In so doing there is a mutual rubbing of his Spirit with our spirit; an engagement so intense permeating every fiber and nerve of our lives.

WORSHIP KEY # 19

'Barrenness' is a product of despising the attitude and heart of worship!

The cessation of adoration is the beginning of a belligerent and complaining spirit. This is breeding ground for doubt and unbelief which are closely linked to lack and barrenness.

WORSHIP KEY # 20

In worship God is the audience; we are the auditioners!

After his creation and redemption accomplishments, God sat down. We his people, through our worship re-tell this story from the instant we are redeemed till eternity; with art and style.

WORSHIP KEY # 21

When you praise you rise and when you rise you become wise!

When you worship, you ascend the ladders of glory and excellence that steady you on a clear course of life; enabling you to navigate its waters with precision and pragmatism.

WORSHIP KEY # 22

Worship is the war-ship you board to go fight life's battles!

Worship is a mystic force with creative and destructive powers. Pointed God-ward, it births life in us; covertly it begets a torrent of divine retribution against the enemy of our souls.

WORSHIP KEY # 23

Worship teaches you to lose focus of yourself!

Worship augments the person of God to levels where more and more of him equals less and less of us. In this equation the self factor diminishes as his Lordship takes root.

Worship demands that you kill some things in your life!

The closer one comes to his light, the clearer their personality-check list becomes. In these intense moments of reverence and adulation, the cry of our heart becomes, "create in me a clean heart oh Lord".

WORSHIP KEY # 25

Worshippers have been sentenced to progress!

Whenever we purpose to hoist the banner of Christ, he reciprocates by drawing both tangible and intangible blessings, triggering a process of consistent advancement.

WORSHIP KEY # 26

Worship is a relation not a religion that requires constant reflection!

The spirit and heart of worship lounge at the heart of God. In this ambiance, a relationship strong and solid is constantly woven always emitting through us spasms of divine awe and wonder.

WORSHIP KEY # 27

Worship is a journey from your place of bondage to freedom!

Worship when compared to a winepress is a place we go tread out the dregs and refuse of life and are filtered as pure and untarnished persons ready to serve our King.

WORSHIP KEY # 28

Your challenges are the exams for your school of worship!

The road map to excellence is tainted with numerous pranks and prickles all of which form a bedrock on which our worship broods and qualifies us for a higher stage of life.

WORSHIP KEY # 29

Some mountains are sorted out when you begin to worship!

Every mountain in our lives has a name. The voice of worship comes to right the wrongs of these towering effigies that pause as indomitable obstacles to our cherished dreams.

WORSHIP KEY # 30

You turn your hell into heaven when you begin to worship!

The rigor and pain that comes with every passing day is a constant reminder of the blissful opportunity we have via our worship to tilt the balance of power in our favor.

WORSHIP KEY # 31

The sole purpose of our creation is worship!

At the inception of the human race through the persons of Adam and Eve, a people were born on the earth realm whose sole purpose was and still remains to worship their creator.

WORSHIP KEY # 32

Worship isn't optional but mandatory!

Like the mandate to reach the un-churched is essential, worship is the modus operandi of getting behind the veil to access Coram Deo. It's the cardinal culture of every kingdom citizen.

WORSHIP KEY # 33

Praise introduces us to God; worship is God's response to you.

Doors swing open as we engage the gear lever of praise leading us into his courts. As we worship, there is an automatic turn around, he personally and magnetically draws us into his bosom.

WORSHIP KEY # 34

Worship is complying with God`s standard.

God feeds on and dwells in the praises of his people. This dictates how we ought to conduct ourselves before him; especially with the quality and quantity of sacrifice we present to him.

WORSHIP KEY # 35

We climb the mountain of God in worship.

Being that God dwells in everlasting burnings, worship births a spiritual pursuit in us that activates a yearning and yelling to behold and lay hold of the object of our adoration.

WORSHIP KEY # 36

In worship, you get caught up in visions of God, entering the realm of answered prayers.

Worship moves you from realm to realm, dimension to dimension unraveling a vortex that separates sensuality from spirituality; enabling you peek into the divine mysteries and secrets of God.

WORSHIP KEY # 37

You can soar above anything on the wings of worship.

Every seen and natural thing is a product of the invisible world. In worship, we tap into the frequency of the unseen world granting us the capacity to override any existing phenomenon.

WORSHIP KEY # 38

Worship is a celebration of God. God will always go where HE is celebrated not tolerated.

Proverbs speaks of better to dwell in a corner of a house than with a brawling woman. As the bride of Christ, he expects and welcomes a heart of gratitude instead of a grumpy and grouchy spirit.

WORSHIP KEY # 39

Worship is the greatest service to God. When we worship him, HE honors us.

The Lord's prayer begins with adoration and ends in adulation. It's the maxima of our prayers. The crown of our sacrifice. Unwittingly it's the renaissance of his favor upon us.

Worship is a sacrifice, releasing what you love and preparing you for your lover!

God is in the accounting business, always drawing from and depositing into our lives whenever we access him. Periods of worship allow us to humbly and willingly let his system take its toll.

WORSHIP KEY # 41

Worship puts you on an exodus to the land of promise.

God cannot stand seeing his people in bondage because he longs for their worship. When we engage in a worship spree we in essence are telling God, "there isn't enough room here to praise you".

WORSHIP KEY # 42

God will always separate worshippers from whiners!

The Almighty has promised to dwell in the praises of his people. The sound of murmuring is an insult to his sovereignty. He will always put a distinction between those raising his banner and the ones tearing it down.

WORSHIP KEY # 43

The purpose of worship is to isolate God to a place where he works miracles!

God feeds on worship, this is his staple food. The scripture says, 'praise is the fruit of our lips.' As we serve him with this choice meal, we are creating an environment for him to be aroused, for our good.

**The signs, wonders
and miracles that happen
in your life are indicators
God is looking for your
worship!**

Throughout biblical history man has sighed and sorrowed under the whip of an age-long tyrant. These beckoning calls have occasioned a merciful God to intervene; triggering an inherent dossier of worship in man.

WORSHIP KEY # 45

In worship,
our deep calls on to God's
deep!

The stockpile of worship that lies within our hearts is often showcased on our lips and body language. When we choose to exhibit it to God, we should do it with all enthusiasm and energy to enthrall his heart.

WORSHIP KEY # 46

Worship is a compellant of change; a propellant to a new range!

Beholding the glory of God through the lenses of worship teaches you that God's nature and attributes never change but his dazzling beauty does. This elevates you to new perception levels.

WORSHIP KEY # 47

Worship is parasitic of God's presence!

Whenever we see the presence of God in scripture, the embodiment of worship is present. From the mobile cherubim in the book of Ezekiel to the stationery ones in the book of Revelation. It's much like horse and rider.

WORSHIP KEY # 48

Worship is the strongest voice of confession!

Every vociferation in worship comes as a declaration of the person, power and promises of God. It's a potent proclamation to the powers that be of an awesome and eternal being; filling the heavens and earth.

WORSHIP KEY # 49

Worship is at its loudest when Passion is at its highest!

Like the biblical-proverbial analogy of a man with a maid, so is worship with our King. The mood we entrance with before his throne, greatly determines the density of incense that emanates from us.

WORSHIP KEY # 50

Worship is the language of divine romance!

Because God's top search list is all about worshippers, there is a dual hormonal upsurge when our antennas of worship are in tune with him. The ancient of days gets engrossed and pitches camp therein.

WORSHIP KEY # 51

The variables of life are corrected in worship!

Questions and queries that permeate our hearts leave gaping holes of uncertainty. In worship these immense voids are filled and fused with his un-changing light and love.

WORSHIP KEY # 52

When worship is nourished, you are flourished!

The contagion of our spiritual and emotional aura is corrected when streams of worship begin cascading therein. This sets off sporadic shifts in our lives that radically effect health and wholeness.

WORSHIP KEY # 53

Petition is prayer in additives; worship is prayer in multiples!

Whereas God permits us to seek him in order to find him, the reverse is true with worship. He seeks those to worship him. When we unleash torrents of our praises, it supersedes what we accomplish with our petitions.

WORSHIP KEY # 54

Worship creates a tender heart BUT models tough hands!

When David slew Goliath, he did it with the rigor and force of his hands; but when he played the harp, the softness of his heart permeated them. Worship very easily mutates the giant in us into a genuflect.

WORSHIP KEY # 55

Whereas Prayer is the language of our spirit; Worship is the music of our spirit.

In prayer a spiritual language is born and incessantly nurtured in us. Through worship, the musical taste buds of our spirit come alive emitting lyrics and chords of magnification and adoration.

WORSHIP KEY # 56

Worship is the foundation of God's throne!

Scripture in the book of Ezekiel bears record to the glory of God being borne by the cherubims. Wherever worship is, God will tabernacle. These are two in separate entities that go hand in hand.

WORSHIP KEY # 57

God has entrusted in worship his attributes!

Worship being all about the heart of God, leads us right into his bosom; where during our intercourse with him, we begin beholding and experiencing the unfolding of his divine attributes.

WORSHIP KEY # 58

Worship feeds into and draws from the source!

We can never out give God. As we endeavor to pour and inject our lives into him through worship, we by default end up supping of his life, power and glory; leaving us invigorated and replenished.

WORSHIP KEY # 59

When worship is stirred, it exudes power!

When the priests were as one to lift up their voices, the glory cloud descended. When we individually or corporately purpose to venerate him, we can't but experience the descent of his dunamis; a free-fall of his potency.

WORSHIP KEY # 60

Worship is our spiritual workmanship!

Humanly speaking, we can never comprehend the form and fashion of a transcendent God. However in worship, the artistry of our spirit begins painting a picture of our King by his Spirit; registering it on our minds and vocalizing it on our lips.

WORSHIP KEY # 61

The genesis of idolatry is the cessation of Worship!

Paul in book of Colossians relates covetousness to idolatry. Our hearts are tailor-made to only and singly covet God. The heart of worship will steadily slip its beat till it stops when idolatry makes its entrance.

WORSHIP KEY # 62

Worship is a diverse and all embracive practice!

John beheld a great multitude of all nations which no man could number. African or Oriental, Infant or adult, rich or poor, learned or illiterate; worship is to be practiced by all in a culture and with a conviction best suited to them.

WORSHIP KEY # 63

The crystallization of worship lies in its composition!

The sensitivity, style and sincerity with which one recipes their worship, will weigh heavy on their end product. Be it a worship leader over a service or a believer endeavoring to cultivate God's presence in their secret chamber.

WORSHIP KEY # 64

Worship is a matrix of a simple yet complex heart!

Worship is patterned and published from the heart. From this vast spiritual organ, an adorning and ornamenting of God takes place with poetry and precision so intense yet with simplistic honesty.

WORSHIP KEY # 65

The reputation of a king is measured by the love of his subjects!

Being such a king who is impartial and with no shadow of turning, worship as our greatest weapon of love comes to illuminate and underscore the magnitude and impact his kingdom has had on us.

WORSHIP KEY # 66

The highway of praise
is the hallmark of power!

Marching around a fortified Jericho city with trumpets of praise projected upwards was a registered symbol of triumph, a victory already secured. God always joins such-like processions and with a grand finale, ends them in style.

WORSHIP KEY # 67

When praise is denied, promises are deferred!

Jehoshaphat is told not to fight, but stand still. He then appoints singers. Every promise uttered over us contains a secret code of praise that carries a command to unleash the standing armies of heaven and set our joy-clock in motion.

WORSHIP KEY # 68

True worship is nectar formed from the crucible of life!

Job arose, tore his mantle and worshipped. David on the other hand exclaimed, 'if the Lord hadn't been on our side'. A life of seasoning in these men and others like them in successive generations has always produced a pattern of sizzling worship.

WORSHIP KEY # 69

Trust is the prime filtrate of your worship!

The barometer of our trust is gauged by a willingness to worship God in the direst of situations. Though cornered and coerced; pressed against a rock and a hard place, yet able to feverishly and faithfully say, "I know my redeemer liveth".

WORSHIP KEY # 70

Obedience is our heart's pace-maker that dictates our worship!

A surrendering of the will is a life-long goal of every believer. Learning to faithfully follow and fellowship in adoration during 'wintery- waiting- periods' is what will sustain you to the finishing line of your faith.

WORSHIP KEY # 71

In the kingdom of God, there is only one throne!

The essence of a throne in a kingdom is power. A seat of justice, judgment and ruler-ship. In the eternal kingdom, the throne is essentially a place of worship. Kingdom citizens discover that their 'rest' is only before this mercy-seat.

WORSHIP KEY # 72

The Trajectory of your Worship will determine your intended Treasure!

Truth is parallel. We harvest what we sow; when we reverence God with our spiritual faculties, we contract his presence. When we worship him with our finances, we partake of his earthly wealth and gold. Depends on your worship avenue.

WORSHIP KEY # 73

When worship condenses, it leaves dregs of joy and happiness!

Continuous joy and happiness are a byproduct of a conscious engagement in a worship picnic thrown out to yourself in and out of season; knowing your adversary is always soliciting your nervous breakdown.

WORSHIP KEY # 74

The word is the lamp of our spirit; worship is the light of our soul!

Whereas the word enlightens your spirit bringing revelation and elevation into God; worship on the inverse prods and provokes the sphere of your soul to cheer up and gear up for Him.

WORSHIP KEY # 75

The scent of worship only flourishes in his presence!

The strength and longevity of any cologne you wear, is determined by its contents and compounder (maker). The aroma of our worship will depend on how much we cultivate Coram-Deo.

WORSHIP KEY # 76

Worship is a tool that fixes satanic chaos!

Knowing he has forever lost the original office, Satan keeps throwing desperate punches on the Saints of God. The best way to pay him in his currency is being fully employed in the position he held... worship.

WORSHIP KEY # 77

Worship is incomplete when bereft of our substance!

The exodus from Egypt was packaged with possessions. Along the way, these belongings formed the bedrock of their service to God. Our journey of life derives meaning when our substance is an integral part of our worship.

Benediction

1Timothy 6:15-16 - *Which in his times he shall shew, who is the blessed and only Potentate, the King of kings, and Lord of lords;*

Who only hath immortality, dwelling in the light which no man can approach unto; whom no man hath seen, nor can see: to whom be honour and power everlasting. Amen.

Jude 1:24 - *Now unto him that is able to keep you from falling, and to present you faultless before the presence of his glory with exceeding joy,*

To the only wise God our Saviour, be glory and majesty, dominion and power, both now and ever. Amen.

Books written:

1. Four faces of a Worshipper.
2. Worship keys for worth-full living

Coming Soon:

1. Nine Elements of Worship
2. Composition of Worship
3. Principles of Faith
4. Seven locks of the Anointing
5. Seven stages of Prayer .
6. Seven significances of the Cross.
7. Art of Prayer.